Built for This

A Young Woman's Journey to Self-Discovery
and Empowerment

KaCey Venning

Published by:

Helping Empower Youth, Inc. 174 Joseph E Lowery Blvd, NW,
Atlanta, GA 30314

First Edition, 2016

ISBN-13: 978-0692626788

ISBN-10: 0692626786

Library of Congress Control Number: 2016901324

Published in the United States of America

Built for This

A Young Woman's Journey to Self-Discovery and Empowerment

KaCey Venning

Dedication

This book is dedicated to my mother, Joyce C. Venning. Since December 29, 2000 you have become more than what I knew I needed. When I couldn't pray for myself, you were there to remind me that you never stopped. Thank you Mommie!

Dear Reader,

As an adult, I reflect on my life often. I think about my childhood in Virginia Beach, Virginia. From the outside, it looked like we had the perfect family: I had parents, siblings and an extended family who loves me. I was born to two parents who were married. My Daddie built a house for my Mommie directly across the street from the house she was born and raised in. That was the story of most of the families in Beechwood. Most of the people who lived there when I was growing up were distant relatives of ours. I just knew everyone was Cousin so- and- so. I couldn't have asked for a better childhood. But even as perfect as things look, life happens to us all. I didn't know it then, but I was starting on a journey to learn what I was called and purposed to do in this life. I was learning what I was built for.

My upbringing really was something out of the movies. There was Mommie and Daddie, my big brother, Daryl and then there were so many aunts, uncles and cousins. I really don't remember having

many friends who were related to me. My childhood best friend, Kamilah, made the cut though. I had so many cousins by the time I finished inviting people to parties and sleepovers there wasn't any room left. This included all of my Halloween-themed birthday parties. There were 5 of us and we were "stairsteps." Bri'Anne was born in 1979, I was born in 1980, Erika in 1981 and Jr. and Alicia in 1982. We did everything together! Trips to the beach and to Disney World and to Niagara Falls, Canada. Trips to Atlanta and all the local amusement parks in between. I can remember summer days and trips to 7-11 for Slurpees and to High's for ice cream.

I can't forget about the cookouts over to the House (the "House" is what we called the home that my Mommie and her siblings were born and raised in. It's the family home). The cookouts were full on productions and everyone had a role! Daddie and Uncle Mac handled the heavy cooking. Uncle Jerome was on BBQ and Uncle Anthony brought the drinks and snacks! Aunt Harriett and Aunt Ophelia covered the sides. Aunt Paulette was on cakes and desserts. Mommie…well, she made sure we had paper products. Aunt Pat made sure everything went according to plan and Aunt Shirley and Aunt Lo made sure everything tasted just right! But the cookouts included live crab boils and it was serious! We had to prep in advance to make sure we had big enough pots, enough Old Bay, some newspaper and the ingredients for the special dipping sauce because we were sure to have a yard full of folks. It looked like a car show out there. Those hot days would turn into long muggy nights, but we didn't care. I can still hear Kim singing Betty Wright in the background while the stairstep cousins ran around catching lightening bugs in our hands. We sucked on butter cups and honey suckles. We picked vegetables from the field so we could snap and shell beans for dinner later. We ate tomatoes sprinkled with salt. And those watermelons were the sweetest I ever tasted.Unk (Mommie's only brother) had the most awesome green thumb; if it could be grown, Unk grew it. It was him and that John Deere, which we all thought was a huge toy and we all demanded rides on the tractor. We played jump rope and hop scotch. We even had our fair share of fights. Oh, the rides in Terrance's convertible 5.0 Ford Mustang or in the back of Daddie's Big Red. Big Red was the Dodge pickup truck that he drove. Back then we could ride in the back and all of the kids would fight to sit on the hump. That's where you would get a big jump if he hit a pothole.

My family and I went to church together where we would hear Aunt Shirley and Aunt Lo sing. And when they got older, it was my older cousins, who are more like my aunts and uncle, Paulette, Wendell, and Ophelia who would sing in the choir. Oh, this reminds me of the Floral Club Family Nights where we would all get together to sing a few selections while Herbie, a close family friend, was on the piano. Dancing under the tent in the yard until we passed out and then watching Earl and TJ walk around in their Tuxedos all weekend from Pernell's and Lisa's wedding because they refused to take them off. Then there were the holidays. There were so many people in the house that most of us ended up on the floor if we were all in the same room. I miss those days. There was so much love around me. We would laugh at Earl's animation when he would holler some insane saying *that only he understood. My family and I created memories and inside jokes that even if we attempted to explain, we couldn't.*

I grew up in a way that I would envy, had it not been my life. I have to admit it was pretty charmed. My cousins and I wanted for absolutely nothing. If we said we wanted it, we got it. It didn't matter who in the family had to purchase it. And that didn't change with Chenell and Nicole either. Alicia had been the baby for so long and when Pernell and Lisa had Chenell, she became the family baby. She was my first baby. I enjoyed babysitting her and having a special bond with her and the excitement continued when I got to the same thing with my second baby Nicole. And while things began to change because Mommie, Daddie, and the aunts and uncles grew older and retired and money tightened a bit, Dejai, Tahjzaneka, Tahjzier and Tazhon haven't been able to get the full effects of a Carroll Family gathering, but they surely cannot deny that they are loved.

Why am I sharing all of this with you? Well, one I love my family and I love talking about them. But, also I want to give you some background about me. I hope that some of the stories I share with you will help you navigate through your own story as a young person. Be sure to read the letters as I wrote them wishing someone shared those thoughts with me at 15 years old. I also want you to read the affirmations. I learned that affirming oneself is essential to success in life. So, make sure you find something to write your affirmations in or on. These are things that helped me and I hope that they help you find your own way to succeed as well. Here is what I know for sure: YOU OWE IT TO YOURSELF to identify and understand how strong you are, mentally, physically, emotionally and spiritually. I can't promise that life won't send some other "stuff" your way, but I can promise that there are tools we can use at any age and at any stage in our lives to take that "stuff" and STAND on it. And while you are standing you can boldly declare, "I AM BUILT FOR THIS!"

Table of
CONTENTS

Built for This Body

You are imperfect. Permanently and inevitably flawed. And you are beautiful.
– Amy Bloom

Picture day at Hermitage Elementary School was always a day full of energy. Weeks prior, we would have received our portrait packages and our parents would select how many of each picture they wanted. This was generally the time where everyone came to school looking their best. You knew exactly when that day was because all the students in the school were on their best behavior with fresh cuts and new clothes to match. Actually, I don't remember much work being done in classrooms as we awaited our class to be called over the intercom to line up in the gymnasium. There is one particular picture day that I remember vividly. My 4th grade class was called into the gymnasium to take our class and individual pictures. Customarily, we were to wait on the side of the gym in a line to be called for our individual pictures. This day is so vivid in my memory because it is one of the few moments that I can recall where I was completely and sincerely confident in who I was and what I looked like. It was a moment I believed myself when I said that I was cute. I had just started to wear my hair relaxed and it was hanging as close to my shoulders as I could get it. I wasn't wearing glasses yet, either. I had on burgundy tights, a burgundy and white knit skirt set. The skirt was a bit fitted and had suspenders that covered my now growing breasts in a striped top. It would be years later before I realized that the picture I took on that day would be my line drawn in the sand about my perception of my body and how much I was beginning to change.

See, I didn't know it then, but that was the start of my body's evolution. I had been VERY skinny up to that point. So skinny in fact, my family thought I was ill because I just would not gain weight. We would visit doctors and they would reassure my parents that there wasn't anything wrong with me. I was just a picky eater, so I didn't eat a lot. My uncle was a cook on the military base at Little Creek and some Friday nights when we were younger, he would bring pizzas to us over to the house. Well, I didn't want anything on my pizza and sometimes I took the cheese off too! And to this day my family still teases me when I eat rice! Mainly because all I wanted was "rice and juice." The juice was whatever gravy or broth was left over from that meal's meat choice. And really that's all I ate. But, puberty took care of all of that and did so quickly! Puberty set in and my hormones kicked in overdrive. I had already begun my period and by 4th grade, curves begin to fill in the lines that had once been my prepubescent frame. Breasts, hips, thighs, and stomach suddenly appeared. While at the time I believed my changing body did not phase me, it became clear that others were beginning to notice, and eventually I would as well.

My Daddie, a carpenter by trade, built me a two-story playhouse. It had become the meeting spot for the kids on the block, if we weren't sitting on the green electrical box down by the corner house. We would gather there to play all kinds of games or just to talk. On a normal day most of the kids were outside on bikes, playing hopscotch, running in and out houses and chilling on the corner. It was the summer time and it was hot. And because at eleven I had the body I would beg God for at twenty-five, I was wearing white short-shorts and a turquoise and white striped tube top, which my C cup more than adequately filled. A good majority of us were playing on the steps of the playhouse when out of nowhere an older cousin snuck up from behind and pulled down my tube top. It felt like time stood still. All of the boys were out that day and wouldn't stop staring. It didn't help that I had a crush on one of them either. I was beyond embarrassed. As I ran into the house pulling up my top, I fell face-first into the couch crying hysterically. My great-aunt, asked me what was wrong. All I could muster was "She pulled down my top!" My great-aunt went to the door and started fussing and of course all of the kids ran away. I stayed on that couch for about an hour before I mustered up enough courage to go back outside.

I just couldn't believe it. I obviously had paid little attention to my breasts, but apparently everyone else had noticed them. As my body continued to grow and expand, so did the teasing. I would hear the whispers and the comments from my "friends" and most of the time I just ignored them. I mean I would be fighting almost daily if I addressed everything someone said to me. So, I just accepted that I had matured quickly for my age and developed the skill of ignoring others' rudeness.. But in learning how to ignore them, I also developed an unhealthy habit of trying too hard to make people like me. The more I was teased about my body, the more I tried to be nice, sweet, caring, kind, and giving. I thought that being nice would deter others' embarrassing comments about my body. So, I was the friend who always bought treats at the store or in the cafeteria line. I became the friend that would do all of the driving or give away clothing or electronics that I loved. All for the sake of being liked. But, as I have grown older, I have learned that isn't the way relationships work. I wasn't aware of the privilege of being selective in my time and good deeds. I didn't know how precious anything I had to offer, be it time or physical gifts given, were and that not everyone deserved my best. I couldn't be all things to all people. But I was determined. It would be a horrible habit to begin at twelve years old.

Reflection:

It's so amazing to me how subtleties creep into your mind and begin to control your thought process. Have you ever experienced that? You may hear one thing that's whispered about you and you find yourself carrying it with you years later. It may be something that you even whispered about yourself. Those times you thought about how unattractive you felt or looked because of a pimple or your own growing breasts and hips. What about when you thought you got it right, by choosing an outfit that made you feel good and you were looking your best and you received not one compliment? How about that whisper of thinking you weren't going to be enough when you had to stand in front of a crowd? We think in error that those things have no merit on our subconscious. But they are seeds that have been planted.

Words have power. When we speak something out loud, our voice is so powerful that the Holy Spirit will conspire to make it happen for us. Our voice and our words carry a vibration that is unique to us alone. So, when we say something, good or bad, the Spirit says, "She is so amazing and so powerful. She gave us a command and now we must make sure that we deliver exactly what she said." That's why when people wake up on a rainy day and say it's going to be a horrible day, what usually happens? It ends up being a horrible day for them. Matthew 12: 34 says, "out of the abundance of the heart, the mouth speaketh" (KJV). This is why a lot of what we do and say is a result of what we have unconsciously allowed ourselves to think about. The things that we allow our minds to focus on are the things we begin to speak from our mouths.

So, as I reflect on my changing body in the 4th grade, I won't say that one incident made me insecure about my body, but it was the sum total of my thoughts and words over the years of not feeling as if I measured up to my family and friend's idea of beauty or popularity that would plant seeds that grew into insecurity and self-consciousness. It would be experiences that would linger with me from the teasing from people who called themselves my friends and older cousins telling me that the boys would want me if I was just a bit smaller. The depressing feeling of not being able to buy what you want to wear because you can't fit it or realizing that although you can get it on your body, you don't look good it. Over the next few years through Middle School and High School I would continue with this same cycle of "buying" friends to mask the pain of the insecurity of being unsure of myself and each year it just got worse. I would continue to gain weight and I continued the cycle of negative self-talk, basically I was bullying myself! I started telling myself I wasn't as pretty as my friends and this would continue my need to overcompensate with my personality. Not only did I continue the cycle of making the universe bring to me these crazy negative things I was speaking, it encouraged the cycle of doing way too much for folks who were undeserving, just so I could be liked and accepted. This is something that I would eventually call People Pleasing. My ill-placed thought was, "If I can keep them happy then maybe they will ignore my flaws and insecurities." Rarely do such accommodations work, if they work at all.

Since my body was growing larger and definitely not getting smaller, I would start to exercise off and on. Before I knew it, I would begin to yo-yo diet. I would lose weight and then gain it back plus some, lose weight and then gain even more the next time. I would hire trainers and would have multiple gym memberships. I would always get really committed and then life would happen and I would stop eating right and working out. . Through reflection I have learned that during those times I stopped taking care of myself it was usually around the time something else was going on that would set my triggers off for depression. I am an emotional eater. I know this about myself. When I am feeling depleted, broken, upset, sad, or tired, I eat. I don't think about it. I just eat. Understanding that and choosing another option requires a level of discipline that is sometimes more difficult than the discipline needed to work out! I had to get this under control. But it wasn't until my Mommie showed me what courage looked like ,that I began to take my health seriously.

My Mommie was diagnosed with breast cancer in 2010. It was a rare form that took a few months to diagnose. Her primary care physician and lead oncologist weren't quite sure what they were looking at. They called in specialists to help them determine exactly what kind of breast cancer Mommie had because its origin of abnormality was unusual. I would call home like I normally do a few times a day and she would tell me about another appointment that she was going to. At first I just shrugged it off as something 65 -year old women do: go to doctor's appointments because they are growing older. I began to get nervous though when she began going more frequently and mentioned that she was seeing various specialists. What made me scared was when she said that one of my aunts was going with her because she needed to have a biopsy done on her breast. As close as my family is, we can also be very private. We try not to let too many folks know what's going on with us.

After lots of tests and consultations with nationally recognized specialists, my mother learned that she had breast cancer. Once she decided on the treatment she wanted and what was best for her, she called me and asked me to come home that Mother's Day weekend in May of 2010. Mommie did say that she was having surgery, but when she asked me to come home, she never explained what the surgery was for. So, we booked a flight for me and I informed my job at the time and my supervisor that I needed a week off to be with my mother. The Sunday before I was to leave, I remember going to my friend's house because we were going to grill and let my dog, Riley, run around the yard. I called to find out if he needed anything from the store and when I pulled up in his driveway, I was in tears. He hugged me through the car window and asked what was wrong. I said "Mommie has cancer". He asked me when she told me and I simply said "she didn't." And she hadn't. I just knew. I know now that it was God's way of preparing me so I could be strong for her.

I went home that Mother's Day weekend. After church that Sunday and our regular family dinner over to the House was over, Mommie and I went home. We were in her bedroom and she said, "Do you believe in prayer?" I told her that I did. She went on to tell me that she had breast cancer and that her surgery was to remove it. I told her that I already knew and that I was in agreement with her that she was going to be just fine. Monday morning we checked into the hospital. Mommie decided to have a mastectomy on her left breast. No chemotherapy. No radiation treatments. She just had it removed, along with the lymph nodes attached. My aunts and her friend Mr. Vernon sat with me. I kept thinking, "What if this happens to me?" My Daddie had died ten years before from complications of prostate cancer. There is a history of cancer on both sides of my family and I couldn't help but wonder what my chances would be for getting cancer as well.

Through research I learned that there isn't anything you can do to 100% prevent any form of cancer, but you can definitely and greatly minimize the risks through diet, exercise and a healthy and low-stress lifestyle. But some things are just hereditary, and this is what kept playing in my head. I decided that I wanted to do everything I could to make my chances as slim as possible. I can't promise that I got it all right in the last five years. Frankly, I have more pounds to lose and better habits to develop in the low- stress lifestyle department. However, I make better choices in my eating and how much physical activity I get. In addition to reducing stress as well. I am proud to say that I have no diseases, no disorders, and no physical conditions. I may be healthy, but I am striving to be healthier. My Mommie made a decision and followed through even though it meant altering her body and her lifestyle. Her health and life were worth it to her. As her body changed, it forced me to consider my own body image and what being and looking like a woman meant to me.

My image of my body has always been one that straddled love and hate. And sometimes I would have these two emotions within hours of each other. I love that I am not a size 6. I enjoy having curves and fullness in my body. But at the same time I don't like the amount of energy I have to use to remind myself of how beautiful I am because I don't fit society's standard of what attractive is. I have learned that as we are all uniquely, creatively, fearfully and wonderfully made, and this includes our bodies, not just our spirits and minds. I have learned that my body bears witness to what I have overcome and accomplished in life. My image of my body does not dictate my perspective of how I show up in the world. I have learned that the more I love my soul and spirit, I begin to take even greater pride in how I dress up this shell that houses the real me, my heart, my mind, my spirit and the love I have been given to share.

I want to remind you that you are built for something special too and that your body deserves attention, love, and care to ensure that it is fit for the journey of you uncovering your passion and your purpose. I hope this letter reminds you of this.

....

Dear Little Sister:

I want you to know how incredibly beautiful you are. Your smile lights up a room baby girl, and your presence means something to those around you. Your ability to pull it all together to look, feel and be your best is a style that is uniquely your own. You take what you have been given and your make it work! Continue to treat your body well. Be mindful of what you are consuming. Fruits and vegetables can be good. Just make sure you balance the chocolate, Swedish Fish, and sodas with things that bring balance to your body and to your mind. You would be surprised at how clear your thinking becomes when you eat healthier and workout. Your body is a temple. It is the house you carry with you everywhere you go. Make it stronger and able to withstand whatever comes your way.

Here's an affirmation for you to declare. Say it until you believe it!

Do you want your body to be strong or conforms to your insecurities?

My body has been fearfully, wonderfully, uniquely and especially made. My body is wonderful, strong, healthy and beautiful. My beauty is not just my body, it illuminates from my mind, my heart and my desire to live my purpose. I treat my body with tenderness and love at all times.

....

Chapter Two

Built to Own My Voice

*Someone has to stand up
and speak for the freedoms of the little guy.
– Christopher Monckton*

Having always been the one called on to speak for an event at church, at work, or in school, it baffles me that I struggled most of my life with speaking up for myself. I admire those people, especially women who have no problem with saying exactly what is on their mind. It is usually my facial expressions that do all the work for me! But, the common thread I have found in these women who speak boldly and unashamedly is that they are usually beautiful and admired by others as well. There's something good to be said about a woman who knows her power and uses it wisely. This is a critical and necessary skillset for every woman, regardless of age, to have. Knowing your own voice and the power it has is not only liberating, but it can be lifesaving as well. Learning how to speak up not just for yourself and others, but learning how to ask for help, redirection and guidance are equally important. Speaking up doesn't have to rude or nasty. Being rude generally doesn't get you what you want anyway. It doesn't always have to be aggressive or dismissive to others. At times, speaking up can and will be very matter- of- fact, without emotion. And sometimes what needs to be said needs to be said softly. However the delivery, your voice must be heard.

Speaking up is simply making your statement known in no uncertain terms about what you need or what you will or will not do or be involved in. Learn how to trust yourself and be okay and comfortable in going against the majority, especially if your opinion or perspectiveis contrary to who and what you are. As you grow and mature, you will find that this quality is one of the most attractive a woman can have. When you know how to speak up it displays a level of confidence in and a commitment to one's self. The ability to speak up allows you to feel good about yourself. Speaking up also is a good indicator to others about what you feel about yourself and this teaches people how to treat you. Believe me; when people know that you are willing to speak up for yourself and against injustice of any kind, they are less likely to bring confusion and disunity your way. They will think twice about trying you. This definitely helps with minimizing the stress in your life. You have less you have to deal with when people think about what to say to you or how to treat you. Even now I sometimes practice in the mirror how I want to say something when I feel as though I have been disrespected or devalued. I need to practice because I don't have a middle ground. My response is either sweet, nice, and fluffy or it's nasty, mean and hostile. I call this my "Zero to 100. I have a "no middle ground" attitude. I do my best to warn people that they don't want me at 100. I remember my experience with a former supervisor. She was assigned to our department without any real world experience in our particular field. She found it necessary to bark orders and make demands without having any prior knowledge of a task or a project. I asked her to refrain from disrupting the team in a very mild and professional manner, both through email and during a rare one on one conversation. She refused. This is where she discovered my "Zero to 100" and I began to explain to her how unprofessional, rude, incompetent, and just a waste of the company's time that she was. Now, that wasn't very nice and is definitely not the part of my personality that I like displayed. But, she didn't quite catch the hint when I was at "zero." Being even tempered helps those who are hostile become more aware of themselves and how much they are over reacting. This will yield to a more positive outcome for everyone. Going to "100" like me, just adds more fuel to the fire, things escalate and become harder to resolve. I haven't quite mastered that even, middle- of- the- road temperament yet. It's something I hope to accomplish soon.

While I encourage people not to push me too much, I have to take full responsibility when I reach 100. How I respond and react is my choice and my responsibility, regardless of what someone else has said or done to me. When I get to 100, it's because I didn't speak up when my feelings were initially hurt. I allowed the offense to speak to my mind and spirit. I internalized it, instead of speaking up and letting it go. When I speak up, I have an easier time in forgiving others and myself and I can work through my emotions a lot faster as well. Waiting until the big blow-up isn't good for anyone involved, especially me. I have made this a priority in my personal development and I have gotten much better at this. My ability to address those who wrong me, right then and there has definitely gotten stronger! One of the things I love a lot about Mommie and my aunts is their ability to put people in their place without having to shout, get rude or use a lot of curse words. It really leaves people scratching their heads and wondering about what just happened. I love seeing that look on people's faces! It completely diffuses the situation and shifts the power and control right back to me. People expect you to get angry, upset and ready to fight when they have disrespected you, annoyed you or showed no concern or regard to your presence or situation. What they don't expect is for you to remain calm, cool and collected. They are not expecting you to respond to them in a way that makes them have to search for a dictionary and thesaurus to understand how you so eloquently just put them in their place. As you continue to grow into your comfortable place in your womanhood, remember, whether it's fair or not, people are always watching you. They have already determined what and who you are supposed to be. Your ability to speak up for yourself in a way that redefines that image is priceless. Not just for them, but for you too. A lot of the pain we experience is self-inflicted, even if someone else has hurt us. Sounds crazy, right? When we don't speak up for ourselves we relive the pain over and over again and it becomes a part of us; that's the internalization I was speaking of. And when something becomes a part of us it begins to dictate how we respond to the world around us. That's just too much control to give someone else.

Have you ever asked yourself why you don't speak up or speak up more often? Could it be that you aren't aware and or you haven't fully embraced your self-worth? Or maybe you feel like you aren't intelligent enough to articulate what you want to say? I had to ask myself all of those questions. My answer came right back to the habits I developed when I was teased about my body. I thought if I spoke up, people wouldn't like me anymore. I was way too concerned about people, who in the grand scheme of things do not matter in me accomplishing my purpose. I wondered if I would lose friends for saying I didn't like something or that something they said or did hurt my feelings. Before I decided that not speaking up was no longer an option, I began to tell myself that these people didn't matter. I pray for them;I wish them well and desire only good for their lives, but that is where I draw the line. They don't get to have a say in how I feel about myself or the added luxury of me considering how they might feel because of my need to speak up. All that is required of me is to be respectful and to not intentionally cause any harm. I had to stop telling myself that saying something to them was a moot point; they weren't going to listen anyway. I was better off just keeping it to myself. But remember, keeping it to myself fostered unhealthy thinking which then showed up in my relationships and in my body and what I presented and gave to the world. There wasn't any other way around it; I had to say something.

But I didn't just start by verbally sharing my thoughts. For those closest to me, I would write letters and I would let it all out. A good friend of mine hurt my feelings when he refused to admit that he had done something that I asked him not to. Because I was still concerned about whether my friends would leave me if I shared my displeasure in their actions towards me with them, I kept my mouth closed and didn't say anything to him. However, it caused me so much stress that when he admitted to apologize, I wouldn't allow him to and then his feelings became hurt by my actions. Writing a letter to him helped me hear myself and it helped me learn how to say what I needed to say without being mean or vicious. The writing helped and it gave me the courage I needed to begin saying it out loud. Speaking up is the best confidence booster there is. It's an outward display of courage that only you can give yourself. But before all of this, the first step in learning how, when and why you should speak up, comes from understanding of why you don't.

Talking is my thing, but talking and speaking up for yourself are very different things. As I have grown older and more mature, I have learned that silence is beautiful too, but only when you have decided that this person's opinion does not further or hinder your growth. Being silent allows you to assess the situation and make an even tempered decision. Every situation doesn't require an immediate response. Learn how to be okay with holding your opinion or your response until you can determine the most effective way of speaking up.

Give me a topic and I promise I can get on anybody's stage and talk until you tell me to sit down! Crowds don't bother me. Yes, I get nervous sometimes, but I am able to overcome. A stage, a microphone and some people… I am at home! This is a big reason why people who are closest to me don't understand why it's so hard for me to speak up. And as much I talk, I have learned that there were times that I wasn't saying what still needed to be said, I hadn't learned how to speak up. Speaking out and speaking up, are two different things, It's what my Daddie would refer to as "you are talking, but you aren't saying nothing!" I remember having to explain to friends and colleagues that talking about something is very different from telling someone they hurt you or asking for something you aren't sure you are going to receive. I can encourage you and give you facts about a point in history or a social injustice and I can invoke an emotion from you easily, but once that's done, I don't have to wonder about the reaction from the stage or a podium in a meeting. Having to go to someone face-to-face and share that you allowed them to control your emotions and thought process is a very vulnerable act and a lot of us are not strong enough or confident enough to place ourselves in those situations. You will begin to see a thread here: my being fearful of speaking up or asking for something goes right back to me not thinking I am worthy of it and allowing my insecurities to control my actions and thoughts. Find someone you trust and ask them to listen. Be upfront with them and let them know that you aren't looking for any feedback at this time. You just need a listening ear. And if you don't have anyone and you need someone to talk to or about something, email me! We all need someone to hear us.

Reflection:

In the last chapter, I talked a bit about body image and the effects it had on me. You already heard the tube top story, but let me tell you about the first experience I had when I wished I was strong enough to speak up. I loved being outside. Sometimes during the summer, my Daddie wouldn't let me outside until the sun started going down, because it was too hot. Mostly because when I would go out, I hated being sweaty and I would take multiple showers. So in an effort to reduce the water bill, he would decide to only let me go outside when it began to cool off. And as much as I love the summer, I loved summers in Beechwood. I can't really call it a neighborhood. It really was one block, and as you remember from the introduction, it was mostly family. My cousins and I would start at one house and weave in between houses and nooks to find ourselves someplace else. The street would be lined with cars of mostly cousins washing and waxing their cars with music blasting from the speakers in the trunk and their girlfriends sitting waiting for them to be done. There were lots of conversations I had with my cousin's girlfriends, and while this was going on, lots of kids riding bikes or playing games.

One particular day I was riding my bike alone and there were no cars lining the street. This wasn't normal but it wasn't scary either. I can't really recall where everyone was at the time. I was riding down the path between two houses on the block.. A close family friend was in his car.His car was white. He let me go down the path first into the street. He eased his car out of the yard and began to drive really slowly next to me. He spoke and I returned his greeting. He didn't say anything else. He just kept driving incredibly slowly. At one point I stopped to see what he was going to do or where he was going to go. He eventually drove off and it left me feeling kind of weird. It's hard to describe. I didn't feel safe and that is what scared me the most considering my block was mostly family. I hadn't felt this way before, so I was unsure what to do about it. He was someone my family considered extended family and wherever my brother and cousins were, there he was as well. There was even a time when we were having a family cookout over in the yard at the house and I went home to grab something. This was not unusual. I mean you can see my house from the yard across the street and everyone was in and out of each other's homes, because back then we rarely kept doors locked. He came in the house to tell me that my Daddie needed me right away. I immediately left. One because Daddie said hurry up and two, I didn't want to spend any additional time in the house with him. I couldn't forget how unsafe I felt when I was alone with him. At ten or eleven I don't know if I really had the words to tell my parents or my brother or older male cousins for that matter, how I felt, especially since he didn't touch me physically and he didn't say anything to me in appropriately; it was just the way he looked at me and the way he talked to me. You know when something isn't right. You know when you don't feel safe. What was I going to say? "He makes me feel weird?"

Through the years I have learned that feeling weird is MORE than enough for you to say something. I wish I would have said something then. What happened though is I began to spare others' discomfort at my own expense. I started to keep to myself the things that made me feel bad or uncomfortable because I didn't know if it was going to be validated or if it was going to make someone else get in trouble or feel bad. Remember the "Zero to 100" attitude I have, this is where it began to take root and I continued with this habit until about two years ago. I still tell people all the time that there is no middle ground with me. It's either 0 or 100. I don't do well with the middle. But I have a better time sharing my feelings now and learning how to become more comfortable in the middle. When I get to 100, I know how to bring it back down to about 70. However, the problem with this before is that I wouldn't let people know when I was approaching 100. I would hold it in for fear of being called emotional or over reacting. I would become irate and emotional because I would carry so much that I would explode! That's not good either. Coupled with the body image issues I had, I didn't speak up for fear that people wouldn't like me anymore. I found myself in relationships and friendships with people who walked all over me. They would take advantage of me and use me. And I let it happen. Because if I was concerned that if I said something, then I ran the risk of them leaving all together, no longer wanting to be my friend. I didn't value myself enough to just cut the string they left in order to pull me back in when it was convenient for them. I didn't take the time to think about how cutting the string would make me feel. I didn't trust myself enough to know that I would push pass the pain and discomfort. Even though being pushed aside after all I have given didn't feel good, at least it was familiar. I always thought I would be the kind of person to have lifelong friends and I envy people I know who have those types of friendships. But as I mature, I have realized and accepted that those types of friendships are not meant for everyone. Be open and don't keep people around, just because they have always been there. It's okay to cut the string. But before I learned this valuable lesson, not only did not speaking up affect my personal relationships but it would carry over to work.

"How do you always end up working for people you are smarter than?" This would be my mother's question each time I shared with her a work-related incident. It was so frustrating! I don't want to be the smartest in the room. I want to learn from others that can help propel me to the next level. My mother's question would come up a lot during one particular position. I worked with people who sat in the room with former and sitting Presidents of the United States of America, but yet the simplest solution or concept eluded them. While it was hard to speak up at work, I found it was an easier place to begin my new habit than starting with my personal relationships. I needed to strengthen my muscle of using my voice for my behalf and benefit. So, at work I began to speak up. It got to the point where work friends would wonder how I was still able to keep my job! I was learning balance and didn't quite get it right all of the time. I prided myself on not being rude or unprofessional. Once I became really comfortable with that, I began to the do the same thing in my relationships. All of them didn't make it. I have lost some friends and will probably lose a few more, but it was worth it.

What is so beautiful about this realization is that I have embraced that my voice has power. It is necessary. My voice is blessed. My voice is invaluable. My voice is the audible source of my spirit. And while I have learned when to be quiet, so I can observe and assess, I have also learned that speaking up for yourself is never wrong or out of place.

I want you to know that you are built to own your voice too! It has power and it's time for you to use it. I hope this letter encourages you to do so.

Dear Little Sister,

It is an awesome display of your strength when you speak loud and proud. It makes those around you so much joy to know you love and respect yourself enough to speak up for what is right and ensure those around you know exactly how to speak to you. The power in your voice is life altering. The ability that you have to speak something and it manifest is awesome. Just remember to always speak life over yourself and the things you want. No longer should you speak doubt or defeat to anything your desire or feel. The power you have to create the life you want is tied to what you speak.

Here's an affirmation for you to declare. Say it until you believe it!

Do you want your voice to be heard or have regrets that you didn't speak up?

My voice has power. It is necessary. My voice is blessed. My voice is invaluable. My voice is the audible source of my spirit. My voice calls forth every good thing I can declare.

Chapter Three

Built to Dance to the Beat of My Own Drum

*Passion is energy. Feel the power
that comes from focusing on what excites you.*
– Oprah Winfrey

One of my fondest memories is getting all dressed up in my leotards and tutus. I can close my eyes right now and see all of the times I went to get fitted for my dance shoes for ballet, jazz and tap. I can remember the photo shoots in the dance studios as we prepared for upcoming recitals with Ms. Lea. Even now, Mommie still has a picture of me somewhere on her dresser in a pale pink leotard, tights, and tutu, complete with my Cabbage Patch baby doll in my left arm. I loved that doll and it went with me everywhere. Those were some amazing times. I enjoyed learning the various eight standard positions of ballet, pirouetting across the floor and doing my exercises at the barre as we warmed up. But then I stopped. I stopped dancing. I stopped doing something that I loved doing and brought me joy. At times I wonder what my life would have been like had I continued to dance. Would I have been healthier, therefore, not having as many body image issues? Would I have been fit and toned? Would I have used dance as a means to create the life I wanted? What would have happened? What happens when we give up on something we love doing? What causes or forces us to let it go? These are questions we ask when we make decisions we later regret.

A lot of times you will hear people tell you to live a life with no regrets, and while beating yourself up about past decisions is not healthy, there will be a few that you do regret making. As much as you can use those experiences to teach you a lesson and allow it to prepare you to make a better or different decision when the opportunity presents itself, sometimes you just wish that you had not made that decision previously. It's unhealthy to walk around ignoring your feelings and the effects of your decisions to save face or to save your pride. Admit it was a bad decision and move forward. Just because you regret or wish you had done something differently doesn't take away from the lesson you learned as a result. Letting go of my dance lessons and later my piano lessons are two decisions I definitely regret. The good thing is that with both of these activities, I can begin again if I want to.

As I have grown older, I have been much more vigilant in making sure that I don't give up on what I love so easily anymore. It's important to have a creative outlet of some kind. I have learned to fight for what I want and if something must change, I find a way to modify, if not let go of it completely. But, sometimes things must take a back seat. There are times when we must let go, but we have to find our way back to them again. Having something to go back to means we had something to begin with. What are you passionate about? What gives you joy and happiness when you are doing it? We all need something that excites us, something we can retreat to when the world becomes too much for us to handle. Sometimes life will make us think that it is too hard to navigate. It's an illusion. We have the tools and resources to get our lives right back on track. Having a safe space to retreat to helps us unlock the tools we need to get back on track.

Grandma's name was Alice and Alice was a character. Being her grandchild was a bit of an experience. You weren't quite sure of what to expect. The older my Mommie gets, the more she acts like Grandma. There just isn't any time at all allowed for foolishness! I was Grandma's last grandchild and although I didn't get to spend a lot of years with her, the time spent was enough to make a lasting impression on me. When I was in pre-K, Mommie would drop me off in the mornings before she left for school. She was an elementary school teacher. Well, Grandma didn't make it out the bed most mornings to meet me at the door. I would get out the car and sometimes Mommie would walk me in, but most times I just walked on in the house, because the door was unlocked. I would drop my book bag off and go into Grandma's room. It's amazing how you can smell memories. Anyway, you remember me telling you how skinny I was? This gave Grandma the perfect excuse to grab me by my arm and fling me across her in the bed. Yes, fling! I am convinced it probably dislodged something in my brain. Her bed was pushed all the way against the wall and this meant that I usually hit the wall and slid down behind her and that is where I stayed until my one of my cousins, usually Earl or Terrance or my brother Daryl, would pick me up to walk me to school on their shoulders as we crossed Northampton Blvd.

As I graduated from Pre-K to half day Kindergarten, I would take the bus to and from school. I went to the morning program at Hermitage Elementary and at 12:30 I would get dropped off at the mailbox. I would run up the long driveway to the red and white house and walked right on. Every day, we had the same routine. I would make a sandwich. Either peanut butter and jelly or a mayonnaise sandwich. Yep, just mayo and bread! I would then sit right in the middle of the floor with a doll and watch TV. The TV as always tuned to Channel 3. Why Channel 3? Because that was the channel that The Young and the Restless was on, along with The Bold and Beautiful, As the World Turns and The Guiding Light. I swear I was the only five-year old in school who had a crush on old Victor Newman. I never even thought to ask Grandma to change the channel. There was so much said in those quiet moments when it was just me and Grandma. The one thing I learned without a shadow of a doubt was she meant exactly what she said and you didn't question it. I watched her remind my older first cousins of what she expected. I watched the level of respect we each gave her without any hesitation. Grandma wasn't the kind who took you in the kitchen to bake cookies, but her love was undeniable and her expectation of our family supporting. Helping and loving each other was to be upheld and acted on regularly.

We were at a dance recital and as I was preparing to go on stage,

I was sitting with my family and the older class was performing. There was this young woman named Sam and even to this day, my family still recalls my grandmother's response, "Now, she know she too big to be on that stage." Grandma was always very clear about where she stood on something and meant every word and deed. Even as I type this, I am wondering how that gene completely skipped me. Anyway, we laughed about it then, but as my body began to change, expand and grow, I would remember what my grandmother said each time I put on my dance uniform and wondered when I would be too big to be on the stage. My body was changing, but maybe had I put my foot down and told my parents I wanted to continue to dance after Ms. Lea's dance studio closed, I would have developed better eating habits and a habit of speaking up for myself. Maybe my metabolism wouldn't have slowed down. Maybe staying active would have saved me from some of the ridicule or hurt I would later endure. Maybe, maybe, maybe... So, really Ms. Lea's studio closing saved me the trouble of having to say out loud, "I quit because I am too big to be on the stage." Yes, Grandma had her way, but I never doubted her love for me. She was born in 1915 and by 1989, she didn't mince words. You took what she said and made it work. Unfortunately, at 9 I couldn't really couldn't decipher Grandma's sarcasm well.

As I write this story, I realize that even from a young age, the opinions of others have always dictated my decision, my direction, and my next move. Becoming consumed with what others thought of me began to outweigh my own thoughts and desires. There were things I wanted to do or say, but I would always filter it through what others would think. What would they say about me? How would they feel about me? Would they still want to be my friend? As each year progressed, I became more and more weakened in my ability to make a decision solely for my benefit. It has caused me to miss out on relationships, experiences and opportunities because I was afraid of what others would say or do. And as much as I have grown from that, I still hesitate for fear of what others might think today. See, part of what makes me unique and special is that I do care about others and their feelings. My purpose is connected to people, especially young people and I am concerned about whether my decisions will hurt or negatively affect those closest to me. However, I have learned that once I have assessed that my decision isn't purely selfish without regard to others, then I am free to move and make decisions as I see fit for me. This realization didn't come easy though.

Reflection:

On October 30, 2010, I turned thirty. I threw myself a fabulous all black masquerade party, invited those I liked and loved and had a great time. But then reality set in. I was unmarried with no children. As the desire to be married with kids continued to consume my thoughts and actions, I stopped and wondered why I wanted these things so badly and I why I had to be married with children by thirty. There were lots of factors. I didn't want to be an "older" mother. My grandmother had my Mommie at thirty and my Mommie had me at thirty-five. I thought to myself "At this rate, I will be forty and I don't want to be near sixty when my children leave the house!" I saw my friends getting married and having babies. I wanted that too; in fact, I still do. But I didn't want to continue putting pressure on myself to meet a certain deadline. I would get all the questions and observations: "When are you getting married?" "You don't have any kids yet?" "Girl, what are you waiting on?" "You better have those babies now." It gets to be a bit much sometimes. The truth of the matter is, if I wanted to be married or have babies just for the sake of having them, I could have been married and have children, then and now. But, my personal desire is to be married before I actively pursue having children. My personal desire is to marry a man who embodies qualities that allow me to trust his character and quest for continual personal growth. I believe that I will be married one day and I will have children. However, I am no longer rushing the process just to please others. I am satisfied with building my own life in my own time. I am excited about how unique I am and that my life was built to be very different from what I see daily. This means that my life isn't going to evolve like others.

If a husband and children weren't going to be a priority in my life at this moment what would I throw myself into? What would bring me joy? It didn't take me long to answer this question: helping others. It makes me proud that I can help make life easier for someone else. I decided I wanted to formalize this. So one of my best friends, Marc, and I got together and decided to merge our individual efforts. He was committed to serving young people by training them and building a skill around the STEM (Science, Technology, Engineering, and Math) curriculum to broaden young people's imaginations to jobs and careers in those areas. I wanted to teach youth how to use their voices to speak to issues that they knew and cared about. In April of 2011, we founded Helping Empower Youth, Inc. (HEY!). HEY!'s mission is to inspire, motivate and mobilize young people to take action that change their world. I wanted to contribute to the world being a better place by providing an opportunity for young people to thrive.

Co-founding HEY! afforded me the opportunity not just to have one or two babies, but hundreds! I was given the blessing of speaking into the lives of young people all over the Metropolitan Atlanta area. There is definitely no shortage of need when it comes to youth and young people! My passion and my future is tied to the success of HEY! and to the success of young people who I have been entrusted to help care for and nurture. Not only does this organization allow me to work with young people, but it also allows me to teach and show adults and other organizations how to do the same. Not only am I working hard to ensure that HEY! is effective each and every day, but I am also taking dance and piano lessons again. It's never too late to return to what you love. Remember, when I said some things you may have to put down and come back and get? Well, I have found the time and the mental fortitude to return to my lessons. I am sure someone might say that I am too big and too old to start dancing again, but I no longer make decisions based on the opinions of others. I make the decisions that are going to keep me happy. Besides, dancing helps to keep me fit physically, mentally, and emotionally and the piano lessons reassure me that I can master anything I want. It helps me keep the beat of my own drum, reminding me that it's okay to do what brings your passion and joy.

What are you empowered to do and to accomplish? What pushes you to want to be great? What are you going to continue to do? What rhythm, beat or sound will you continue to dance to in life? What gives you joy?

It is my sincerest desire that you move joyfully through life, dancing and laughing. I hope that my letter to you encourages you to make that drum beat loud!

....

Dear Little Sister,

Get into it! And get into it with all of your heart. You are too talented, intelligent, bright, funny, creative and needed to sit at home and not let the world experience the awesome gift you have to give. We all have something that piques our interest, something that excites us each time we think of it. Have you decided what that "it" is for you? If not, I encourage you to do so. It doesn't have to be expensive or difficult. I don't even care if it's coloring! Find something that makes your soul stir and brings a smile to your face. Then I want you to do that each and every time life decides to want to test your strength. Have something you can go to that will take your mind off the things that are weighing you down and making you sad. Just make sure that the "it" you choose is something that means you and your spirit well.

Here's an affirmation for you to declare. Say it until you believe it!

Do you want a song that is unique to you or to dance to one that everyone else dances to?

I am creating the life that I want and it is beautiful!
....

Chapter Four

Built to Thrive

*My mission in life is not merely to survive, but to thrive;
and to do so with some passion, some compassion,
some humor, and some style.*
– Maya Angelou

Being a teen and a young adult is hard work. Really, I think more young people should be applauded for their ability to make it through adolescence without losing their selves or their minds completely. I barely made it, and that's no exaggeration.

It was January 26, 1997 and the New England Patriots were playing the Green Bay Packers in Super Bowl XXXI (31). I can't remember exactly what quarter we were in the game or even a moment that made me upset, but I found myself upstairs in my younger cousin's bathroom with the door locked. The youngest stairstep cousin came to the door and began asking how long I was going to stay in there. I mean, we had been having a great time. We had chicken wings and chocolate cake (an old family favorite); a house full of family and close friends; football pools with dollar bets; merriment, laughter, and memories being created. For some reason, I still found myself in the bathroom with the door locked. When asked how long I was going to be in the bathroom, I replied, "I don't feel like anyone loves me and I want to die." Thank God, she didn't think that I was being melodramatic and went to get my parents. Instead of going home, we went straight to the Emergency Room at Bayside Hospital. A few nurses and doctors came in and out to assess whether or not I needed to be placed on suicide watch or admitted to the psych ward. Once they determined that I was not going to be a danger to myself or my family, they sent me home with explicit instructions for my parents to make an appointment for me to see a therapist. My mother called my aunt to get a referral and off to the psychiatrist we went.Although my upbringing and childhood were quite amazing, something didn't always click for me. I didn't always feel the obvious love around me. After my declaration of feeling unloved, the outpouring of love increased and I still could not feel or accept it. As much as people told me--and showed me--they loved me, I couldn't see it. I just did not feel loved at all. Once I saw my psychiatrist a few times, we learned that I had a chemical imbalance in my brain. Basically, a chemical imbalance is the soft blow to patients and their families, when the doctor really wants to explain a more complex diagnosis. What I would later learn is that I have to live my life with the symptoms and consequences of major depressive disorder with paranoia and anxiety. Sounds like a lot, right? Well think if my psychiatrist had given me and my parents this news when I was sixteen? Because my symptoms and my episodes were mild, the doctor didn't want to make the situation worse. He prescribed some pills and sent me on my way.

I was out of school for about a week or so mainly because my Mommie didn't want me to feel pressured to do anything that would cause me any stress. So I stayed home and rested. I returned to school still filled with anxiety. Then there was that time when I was in church sitting next to my aunt and all of sudden I felt overwhelmed. I left the sanctuary and went to the office where my Mommie was and just started crying. For some reason I felt anxious sitting next to my aunt. All she said was "Hello." Mommie calmed me down and sent me right back into church. In hindsight, all of this sounds really crazy, right? It does seem like it is a lot going on. What I learned is that there isn't any right or wrong environment for you to feel how you feel. What is important is that you understand what you are feeling, your triggers and how to keep moving forward. I learned how to identify my triggers by going to therapy and by being honest with myself about how something made me feel. I realized that I didn't have to share this thought with anyone, That realization alone made it safe for me to admit what I did and did not like and why. Once I was made aware of those things, I could sense and identify sooner when something would make me upset. It helped me prepare for the recovery more effectively.

What I would later learn is that my feeling unloved wasn't the fault of those who loved me or even my fault. It was simply some wiring in my brain that decided it didn't want to work properly all of the time. Once I learned more about my diagnosis, I began to feel better. I realized that I had to work a little harder, but it would be worth it to feel the love that was so freely given to me. I wanted to live, I wanted to thrive. And while, I have had other low moments and I might have others in the future, I know that I can rebound and continue forward with my goals.

Learning my triggers has been most helpful to me. They are the signs that I respond to in order to pull back or away from people or environments. I know personally, I cannot over commit myself to others and events. When I take on too much, it becomes too much for me to handle and I have these min-meltdowns. I will shut down and will do nothing at all, not even the necessary. Being an overachiever isn't beneficial if you aren't able to do all things well. Learning how to complete one task at a time and be a high performer versus an over achiever, has been a life saver, literally. Now, I make sure that I laugh every day. I have learned how to laugh until my soul flourishes. I surround myself with the people who I KNOW love me and want me in their lives. I say no, a lot. I exercise and talk to my Mommie daily. I pray, a lot. And then I pray some more. I remind myself of who I am and what I am built to accomplish. I sing and listen to music. I have found the things that immediately bring peace to my spirit and I ensure that those things happen daily.

Reflection:

Finding your own "recipe" of how to manage your triggers and how to recover will work wonders in your life as well. I might have to take medication for the rest of my life and I am okay with that, but I know what else I have to do in order for the medication to work optimally. No one desires to walk around like a zombie, unable to feel anything. Numbness is not the answer. Shutting down and ignoring life is not the best response either. Being able to self-manage in conjunction with medication may increase your ability to learn more about yourself and how to make the best of the situation at hand.

Mental Illness is no longer a death sentence. To be honest, it still has a stigma attached to it. No one wants to admit that something is wrong outside of their control. And there are so many people who think that having a mental illness is an excuse to behave in a way that is full of emotional outbursts and irresponsible actions. Believe me; no one with a mental illness wants to act "crazy." We don't sit around thinking of ways to show out, well not all of us. While it may still be something people don't want to admit they struggle with, there are so many people walking around undiagnosed. Now, let me be clear. I am not one of those folks who assume that every issue can be categorized as a mental illness. Sometimes life is just hard and it forces us to respond in ways that wouldn't necessarily be our first choice in a calm and more rational environment. But there are so many who really do have undiagnosed illnesses, mostly because they don't want the label. Having a mental illness is no longer an automatic life-long sentence to an insane asylum. It doesn't even mean that you will need to take medication daily. I know plenty of people with very real mental illness diagnosis who do not medicate at all. I do, and I am okay with that. The stigma attached to mental illness keeps so many of us in a perpetual state of fear: *What will people think of me if they knew what I struggled with? Will they think I am crazy? Will they treat me as if I am crazy? Will they stay away from me? Will they love me or will they think I am too much to handle?* These questions have caused me to make so many bad decisions related to work and relationships. I allowed these questions to guide my decisions. So, I alleviate all of those questions from my mind, by being upfront with those who matter. I have learned my triggers and my recipe for emotional success: I pray, I take my meds, I work out and I live my life, but mostly I pray and in my prayers I am reminded that God is big enough to handle even my emotions. This gives me personal permission to give it all over to Him and to allow Him to fix whatever I think is wrong at the moment. There are times when my prayers are 5 minutes and I immediately feel peace and then there are times when I find myself praying all day, just begging God for a bit of release from the emotional turmoil. What I can say for sure is that each time, He comes through for me. And when I get up off my knees from praying, I give thanks for my diagnosis, It's sounds crazy, doesn't it? To thank God for a mental illness diagnosis? Well, knowing my diagnosis has given me great freedom. It has allowed me to live.

It is my sincere desire that you are mentally healthy and if you are the best way to stay there is by having regular healthy outlets to reinvent yourself and re-energize. Remember to find something that you love doing. Find someone that you trust and can confide in. Don't get in the habit of telling all of your business all of the time, but find someone that is going to lovingly help redirect you or just listen. If there isn't anyone that you trust, find a licensed and reputable therapist, even a minister or school counselor. And then I encourage you to pray or mediate. That voice that lives within you will always listen and you will learn more about yourself and your purpose from that voice inside of you as it will guide and direct you to the right path.

Don't be afraid of the thoughts in your head or your feelings. Trust yourself enough to choose someone to share your thoughts and feelings with. Let them remind you how incredible you are!

Dear Little Sister,

It is okay to go and talk to someone. Actually, I believe everyone should see a therapist at least once a year. Seeing someone who is objective allows for you to hear a different perspective and view about yourself and your life. Embrace the opportunity to share your deep dark secrets with someone who isn't going to judge you or treat you any differently upon hearing what you have to share. Going to therapy has been helpful and rewarding. I get to say all of the things I want to say to others without having to hurt their feelings. I also learn different ways to cope with what bothers me the most. Don't be afraid, get excited about it. If the thought of seeing a professional is too scary right now, find someone you can trust completely.

Here's an affirmation for you to declare. Say it until you believe it!

Do you want to be a young woman who is strong enough to admit her weaknesses or succumb to them?

I am thankful for a peaceful mind. I am grateful for the power of love and strength that I walk in.

Chapter Five

Built to be Great!

Life isn't about finding yourself.
Life is about creating yourself.
– George Bernard Shaw

Living up to everyone's expectations can make you feel as though you really haven't accomplished anything at all. And that is a horrible feeling especially, when the expectations are pretty high. Then there is the pressure that you may feel when the expectations are high, or ones that you wouldn't set for yourself. I had a conversation with afifteen-year old once and he mentioned to me that he didn't like to hear that adults had high expectations for him, that it was too much pressure to ensure that he measured up. I shared with him that I understood exactly how he felt, but that high expectations are given to those who have capacity and ability to meet them.

Expectations are defined in <u>Webster's Dictionary</u> as "a strong belief that something will happen or be the case in the future." It is also defined as "a belief that someone will or should achieve something." This second definition is the one most of us find ourselves trying to live up to. Whether we recognize it or not and definitely whether we like it or not, we are constantly living up to expectations. The problem is we are usually living up to the expectations that others have set for us, and not those we have identified for ourselves.

Having great expectations can be an awesome thing. It is that push that we need at times. I know for myself that I do better when I know someone is counting on me to do something. It gives me the energy I need to dig a little deeper when my own self-motivation is lacking. But, it becomes problematic when the only expectations you have are those that others have been created or defined for you. There will be times when you aren't up for doing what others want you to do and feeling the guilt of letting them and in turn yourself down. At least I know I do, and suffering with the guilt imposed by others is no fun. My own guilt has been enough.

As I was coming to terms with having a chemical imbalance that triggered Major Depressive Disorder for me, I remember having a conversation with an older cousin. We were at a family cookout when she asked me why I felt I was unloved. I gave her a very ill-thought out answer. I replied "Because people always want something from me. I feel like I am being used." Her response was "KaCey, we aren't using you. We trust you." She explained that because I was a leader and am trustworthy, the family knew they could call on me to get things done without having to worry about whether or not the task would be accomplished. I guess even at sixteen, I was in the makings of becoming a fixer, someone who solves other people's problems, to folks around me. My cousin didn't want me to see being a leader as a burden or something to run away from. She wanted me to take pride in knowing that others thought of me as mature, responsible and as one to count on.

While my cousin's confidence in me helped, it didn't make dealing with the pressure of performing any easier. I still felt this insurmountable pressure to make sure I did everything that was expected of me, even when I didn't feel like it. The need to perform also tied into my insecurities that were beginning to overtake my life as well. By now, I was heavier than most of my friends and cousins. Not only did I have this mental health diagnosis, but I was also experiencing the beginning symptoms of PCOS (Polycystic Ovarian Syndrome). PCOS is a clinical disorder that triggers an abnormal imbalance in your female hormones. It can not only affect your reproductive ability, but also trigger insulin resistance if not watched closely can turn into Type 2 Diabetes. While I didn't know it at the time, I would later be diagnosed officially with this disorder. The effects of PCOS made it hard to lose weight. I also began to experience discoloration in my face, which threw my hormones into a frenzy each and every day. So here I was a hormonal teenager with a mental health diagnosis and a medical condition that tripled the negative effects of the hormones in my body. I was a wreck waiting to happen! Having to deal with all of this internally, plus my "people pleasing disorder" that I created to try and simplify my life, was too much! I reasoned if I didn't have to figure out life on my own and just do what others expected of me, I had one less thing to worry about. But being young and naïve, what I failed to realize is that I gave others permission to determine what success and accomplishments looked like in my life. And when I didn't live up to their expectations, they felt the right to inform me of their disappointment. I fought hard to make sure people around me weren't disappointed. I wanted them to love me and like me and I would do whatever was necessary to make sure that happened, even at the expense of my own happiness, peace, health, finances, and goals.

In January 2004, I decided to move back home to Virginia Beach from Atlanta, GA. At this time, I had done all I could do to maintain my sanity. I was working a part-time job in the mall, a was a college dropout and was incredibly unhappy. I gave up and went back home. . By now, I think Mommie knew I needed a break. Instead of telling me to stick it out and not make a decision to move home out of fear or sadness, there wasn't any push back this time. She simply reminded me that I could always came home, so I did. I went home and began working full time in the local school system. I also took a few classes at the local community college. I felt like I was finding me, for the first time. Now, everyone wasn't very happy about my decision to move home. The family I had created in Atlanta felt as if I was abandoning them. At the same time, I was very concerned about what others at home in Virginia Beach would think about me moving home with no degree, no job and no real plan for my life. They might have understood it more had I moved back home with a husband or a baby. But I came home with nothing. At this point, I didn't care. I just needed to be some place safe. The house my Daddie built is always safe for me. It was literally built with his two hands and it is where Mommie and I retreat when the world is too much to handle.

By March 2005, I was feeling the itch to move and shake! I decided to return to Atlanta. But, I knew I couldn't return without a plan. As I began to search for jobs, I came across the opportunity to serve in AmeriCorps. AmeriCorps is a nonprofit program that provides grants to local and national organizations to encourage civic engagement in issue areas such as education, public safety, homelessness and health. Serving as an AmeriCorps member gave me the opportunity to work full time in the Atlanta Public School System, volunteer and learn about nonprofits. I began researching the steps to join the HandsOn Atlanta School-based AmeriCorps Program. It proved to be one of the BEST decisions I made for myself. I count it as an awesome decision because while the position didn't pay much, it would be steady and provided access to the Atlanta Public School system, the Greater Atlanta nonprofit community, and I could earn education awards to use to return to school without having to use loans. It was a win-win for me. I applied and I was accepted as a Team Leader, which gave me the opportunity to earn a bit more money per week. Mommie volunteered to help with the rest of my needed budget to make sure I wasn't stressed and could find a way to enjoy living. In July of 2005, I returned to Atlanta.

Reflection:

Moving home and then moving back to Atlanta taught me that when I can identify for sure what it is that I want to do, there is no stopping me! It's easier for me to ignore the naysayers. I have a better chance at finding happiness and peace, even if something doesn't work out the way I planned. I have learned to say no and mean it. I have also learned that I don't have to share everything with everyone. This realization came about when I noticed that I was unmoved by someone's disapproval of a decision I made. I actually was excited that they were disagreeing with me. It helped to foster an environment where I am no longer looking for the validation of others. Therefore, giving them room to have an opinion on my life is no longer an option.

I encourage you to lead and not follow. But that means learning to lead yourself as well. It can be so easy to just do what others expect of you. When you follow, you do a disservice to yourself; you owe it yourself to learn who, what and whose you are, so that you can begin to set your great expectations.

I pray this letter helps you realize the greatness that lives inside of you.

....

Dear Little Sister:

Your life is yours to create, so dream big! I am a firm believer that if we have been allowed to think of something regardless of how big, grand or seemingly impossible it is, it is something that we can achieve. I would hate to believe that our imagination and desires are cruel jokes. While it's a good thing to know others want the best for you, you have to want the best for yourself as well. How badly do you want the life you dream about? Wanting it isn't enough; you are going to have to work for it. I promise that even though the work may be hard, it is going to be well worth it! Set your own expectations for your life, but make them good. And make them something that you can look back on in 10, 20 or 50 years and still be just as proud as you are today!

Here's an affirmation for you to declare. Say it until you believe it!

Are you going to allow others to make decisions for your life or will you use your power and lead yourself?

I expect only great things to happen in my life. I expect to succeed.

....

Chapter Six

Built for a Mother's Love

*Whatever else is unsure in this stinking dunghill
of a world a mother's love is not.*
– James Joyce

Debutante Balls. You either love them or hate them. I can see it now, the long white gowns, with the long white gloves and white stockings and white shoes. Then you have the ballroom dancing and the presentation of Debutantes. Blah blah blah. I didn't quite care for my experience. I understood the hoopla surrounding them. If you are a member of Middle Class Black America, it's almost a must if you have the chance to participate. Between the workshops and classes at the Virginia Beach Central ibrary and the fundraising I was in preparation mode. This is my introduction into society. This was my family's public opportunity to say they raised me right and that I was now ready to make my own mark in the world. However, historically this was also a way for parents to let acceptable suitors know that their daughter was of marrying age soon. But since I wasn't being betrothed to somebody's son, what was the point in 1998? Now that I think about it, it was a chance to dress up, raise money, dance, eat and be merry.

I wasn't surprised when my mother said I was going to be a debutante in 1998, my senior year of high school, but I definitely was not excited about it. I really could have cared less at that time. But, if you know my mother, you know that if she says you are doing something, then basically it is already done. There was absolutely no use in using any energy or words saying otherwise. I don't remember making any decisions surrounding this event at all. As a matter of fact, my high school boyfriend wasn't even my escort. As mothers often do, she made an executive decision and chose someone else. I believe I saw the dress I was wearing a week or two before the event and that was because it needed some slight alterations from when my older cousin wore it the year previously. Mommie chose my hairstyle, the shoes, etc. I basically just showed up.

My mother is a picture-perfect example of a Gemini. When she is laughing and having fun, there is no denying it and then in a moment she can be really serious and give you that "I ain't playing with you" face. Friends always tell me how nice and sweet my mother is. My reply, "yeah, but give it a minute." So, I was a bit confused that night because she could not and would not stop smiling. I think subconsciously I wondered what I needed to do to make her smile like that all the time. I must admit, I had a grand time at the ball. I still am not feeling that dress to this day, but deep down *I* felt good. My escort was a perfect gentleman and someone I knew from church so we had a good time. My Daddie was a show stopper for sure! Daddie was definitely the oldest father in the room and he had two left feet. But, he shined when the spotlight was on him. He knew how to make the people feel good. I remember Mommie sharing a story in her book, Daddie <u>The Old Man and the Doors,</u> about how she knew where my father and I were in the room by the laughs, smiles, and people standing to get a good look. I kept trying to get my father on beat, in sync, but I gave up when I saw how much fun he was having and how much the people in the audience enjoyed seeing him dance with his baby.

Before the activities necessary to prepare for the Debutante Ball, I knew that I was attending Morris Brown College in Atlanta. I was ready and anxious to go. So, letting Mommie have her moment with me May of 1998 was well worth it as I would be off to college soon. In August of 1998, I began attending classes as a Freshman and one day, I called and asked Mommie why didn't she help me get into college. Yes, I had been accepted and was attending college, I was a bit annoyed at the fact that I "seemed" to have done it all by myself. I was listening to stories of friends who had people help them fill out applications and make decisions. My experience was that all of this had been left up to me and I was a bit insecure about whether or not I had made the right decisions. Mommie listened until she had heard enough. She then very sternly told me, "If I had done all of that you wouldn't know how to make a decision for yourself, positive or negative consequences aside." She went on to explain how she wanted me to be a leader, to learn how to be confident in what I wanted and needed so that I could make decisions without others. While, I heard her and I understood, I still didn't like knowing that I wasn't confident enough in myself to be okay with my decisions.

Reflection:

Life happened and I was in and out of college for a long time. After I had returned to Atlanta in 2005, I thought I was on the right track, but I remember having a crying fit one day in 2009 because I just didn't feel like an adult at 28 ,and I called home to my Mommie. I began telling her through sobs and hiccups that I felt like I was a burden to her and that I just didn't know what I was supposed to do to get on track. Mommie always gets really frustrated with me when I start doubting myself, and while I try to hide my annoyance in my voice, she does not. Mommie shared with me that she is always proud of me. She went on to tell me that while she isn't always excited about the decisions I make, all she wants is for me to be honest, to try my best and that is all she ever expects from me. She further explained that her job as my mother was to provide and care for me for as long as it was necessary. She just wanted me to have the tools and resources to be great. My Mommie and I weren't close growing up and it has definitely been since my father's death that we have grown as close as we probably could be. Knowing this has helped me learn how to accept, appreciate and pay attention to my mother's love in a way I would have normally otherwise ignored. What I realized is that I didn't have to be perfect. And that revelation alone has been enough for me to be okay.

By understanding my mother's unconditional love for me, I have found my own for her. I am so very protective of my mother and when I believe others are doing her wrong, I take it personally. I want to fight for her and my sincerest desire is to give to her. I long for the day, and I am working towards it, where I can say "Mommie, check your account. I just made a $10,000 deposit." And that $10,000 is only the beginning. I can't wait for the day when her birthday or Christmas present, is the deed to her house, because I paid off the mortgage. That day is going to be awesome! I want her to have the ability to keep her retirement check, and spend it how she sees fit and not on the necessary and mundane. My desire to give to my Mommie is a meager attempt to give her a physical display of my appreciation and gratitude I feel for her being my mother. Growing up she may not have been my friend, her words were "I am your parent and not your friend. We can be friends when you become an adult, "but she was an awesome parent, who set standards, expectations, and an example of what she desired for me to become. I am so glad now that she is not only my Mommie, but one of my best friends.

Mothers can sometimes annoy us to no end, but when we allow them to teach us by words and examples, we learn exactly what not to do and more so what to do more of. I hope this letter encourages you to strengthen your relationship with your mother or someone who is like a mother to you.

Dear Little Sister:

Mommies can definitely get on our nerves! I think it's some unwritten rule that they have to be mean at times. What I have learned though is that most mothers find their own way of loving their children and their desire is for their children to be okay. Yes, sometimes they have expectations of what it is that we are to accomplish and what kind of women we are supposed to grow into. But in reality, all they want is for us to be healthy and happy. Everything is extra. Give your Mommie some room to make mistakes. Learn how to strengthen your communication with her. Mommies know how to give us just what we need. Take advantage of her unconditional love, by giving some of your own.

Here's an affirmation for you to declare. Say it until you believe it!

Do you choose to accept your mother's love or will you choose to fight against it?

I am the daughter of a woman who loves me beyond measure. I am proud to have a mother who cares for me and wants the best for me.

Chapter Seven

Built to Take Risks

*You can't get anywhere in life
without taking risks.*
– Esme Bianco

We find comfort in what we know. It's natural to have an attachment to what is familiar. But have you ever thought of doing something different? Sometimes we miss out on really good things because we are unwilling to leave what is familiar, to leave what we know. I am not a huge risk taker. I don't like roller coasters or heights. So, when my friends and I went to Belize on a trip and they went zip lining, I allowed my fear to overtake me and I missed to the opportunity to zip line in this amazingly beautiful Caribbean country. I make mention of it because I forgot to tap into the courage it took for me to leave Beechwood to attend college in Atlanta. That took courage for me. My family has always been my safe space and leaving them was definitely scary, but I was also excited about the possibility of meeting new people and experiencing new things. Even, taking my first international trip required me to leave the familiar.

Traveling internationally opens your eyes globally for sure and I think that everyone should have a chance to leave the comfort of not only their city and state, but their home country as well. I was so sacred. Would I understand what people were saying to me? How would I navigate the area I was in should something happen? See, I know the answers to those questions living in the United States of America. I didn't know them in Belize. But guess what? I went anyway. Leaving what is familiar doesn't just have to be travel. Sometimes leaving what is familiar is about your mindset or your thought process. It could be the toxic friendships and relationships. Who are those people in your life who have a hard time encouraging you or speaking positively over your life? You may have to distance yourself from them. You must be willing to leave what you have always known, especially if it isn't good for you. But, also sometimes it is good to leave what has been good too. Far too many times we get too comfortable in what feels good and we miss out on something greater and better. Ever heard the phrase, "Good, better, best. Never let it rest, until your good becomes your better and your better becomes your best"? It's so true. Don't let your good become enough. Always work towards your better and then your best.

Reflection:

I had to remember all of these things when I decided to leave home at seventeen to attend college. It was a huge step. I was leaving my family, my friends, my church and my beloved Beechwood. But I was ready, even in my fear. I wanted to see something different. I received encouragement from everyone. My family and friends were excited to see me spread my wings. But, they didn't hide the fact that they would miss me and it made me feel good that in spite of them missing me, they still wanted me to go. So, I thought.

I later learned that not everyone was okay with this decision and as much as they said that they were excited, chatter behind my back sounded like this, "Why does she have to go to Atlanta? Is staying home not good enough for her?" Now, I could have allowed this to keep me home. But I ignored it and realized that I had to make this decision for myself. After my second year of school, I had an encounter with a family member who feared I thought I was better than the rest of the cousins. This relative felt I was getting extra attention from our aunts and regretted that she didn't have the opportunity to do what I was doing. I wish you could see my face even now. I was very confused because every opportunity I had, was afforded to all of my family. There wasn't anything that

I was doing or being supported in that my other cousins could not have experienced as well. What I am grateful for, is that this confrontation didn't break the bond of family. We got past it.

After Daddie passed and I decided to return to school after taking a semester off to be with my Mommie. I was a little scared that I was making a bad decision in taking a semester off. Would this be a failure in my life that I couldn't rebound from? But not only was I afraid of making the bad decision of not returning to school, I was also concerned about how we were going to pay for my tuition. Attending Morris Brown meant I had chosen a historically black college and it was a private school. I remember tuition in 1998 was already over $18,000 per year. I wondered how my Mommie going to pay that without student loans. And each time I brought it up, Mommie would tell me not to worry about it. My only job was to return to school and do what I was supposed to do. I later learned that Mommie had help from some family members. They stepped in and worked together with Mommie to get my tuition paid. Not only did my family chip in to help me with school, but they made sure I returned home for every family event, holiday, and break. This might have been my older cousins were driving me to and from Atlanta, my stairstep cousins were driving with me to keep me company on the road or one of my aunts helping Mommie with the purchasing a plane ticket for me. These small gestures and acts, are actually pretty big I don't know if I would have learned to appreciate my family and how close we are if I hadn't left home. Leaving home gave me the space and the time to see how much my family loves me and misses my presence.

It's okay to be a cautious of a new experience. But don't allow fear to keep you from spreading your wings. Remember fear isn't real. Danger is, but fear isn't. Fear is simply a reminder that we have never gone this way before. And that's okay. I pray this letter encourages you to take risks!

KaCey Venning | 61

Dear Little Sister:

I want you to know that you have wings built inside of you. Some of us locate them and use them earlier than others. Then, there are some of us who need a little help finding them. Finding your wings will require you stepping outside of your comfort zone. Be afraid to fail. I fail all of the time and I LOVE it!! Seriously, I call it Failing Forward. When you step out to do something different, there is always a chance that you aren't going to get it quite right. That's what your wings are for. Either they are going to take you to your next level or help you fly back home. Your life isn't a race that you must finish on someone else's time table. There isn't anything written that says you must do anything in a certain order or in a certain time. The goal is for you to just keep moving. You have to be like Pumba and Timon in <u>The Lion King</u> and sing "Hakuna Matata" For you have no worries, for the rest of your days. Use it as your problem free philosophy. Yes, of course things will come up in our lives that will make us upset or get us off course, but if you remember that there is a larger plan working on your behalf, you can let the stress and worry go and just keep moving! Take a chance. Spread your wings and fly. Even if you don't make your destination on the first trip, use your wings to return home and get refueled to try again. Get comfortable with being uncomfortable. Be okay with doing something different. Trust yourself enough to try. You can do this by building a network of people who support and love you. They will help to cushion to fall when you begin to fail forward.

Here's an affirmation for you to declare. Say it until you believe it!

Are you okay with allowing fear to determine your future or will you look fear in the face and say "you do not matter?"

I want something different and I am not afraid to risk it all to get it.

Chapter Eight

Built to Stand My Ground

*Everything will change. The only question is
growing up or decaying.*
– Nikki Giovanni

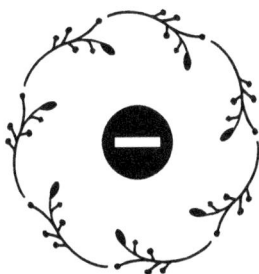

Learning to become an adult is an ongoing process. Believe me! It's so funny to me to hear my Mommie tell me that someone asked about "the baby." My response is "tell them the baby is grown!" But to my family and my church family back in Virginia Beach, I am always going to be the baby. When people continue to ask my Mommie about me and why she thinks I decided to stay in Atlanta vs. returning home, she always tell them that Atlanta is where I came of age. And it's true. Atlanta is where I learned about what kind of woman I wanted to be. I began to research my family's cultural ties and what my connection to history is. I tapped into my purpose. Coming of age means so many things to people, but really it's about when you begin to find out who YOU are, what and who you want to be and you begin to make decisions for yourself. Moving to Atlanta and attending Morris Brown College did all of those things for me. But, it wasn't without a fight.

Arriving at Morris Brown College threw all of my insecurities in my face! I mean EVERY SINGLE ONE of them. To be honest I wasn't prepared or equipped to handle them maturely. I found myself in a few compromising and dangerous situations. I remember visiting a guy in the attached dorm. I wasn't really feeling him. I definitely was not attracted to him but I found myself bored that day when he asked me to come over. It was a Saturday afternoon and it was pretty quiet. Most people were out and about and it was rare to find most folks on campus on a Saturday afternoon.

So, since I didn't have anything to do, which probably meant that two people I spent the most time with my Freshmen year were someplace with their off campus boyfriends, I was left to entertain myself. Even writing this is sounds like an awful excuse. Anyway, I went to this guy's room. I don't even remember his name. We were supposed to just watch TV. Well, since I already wasn't remotely attracted to him, I definitely didn't want him touching me in any form or fashion. When he did, I politely asked him to stop. He didn't. As a matter of fact, he became even more aggressive. At this point I began to become scared. I started to wonder how far he would take my rejection Even though I knew no one else was on his hall, I decided my best bet was to scream and start to talk really loudly. I hoped that would convince him to stop for fear of someone hearing me. Well, he cared not. He continued to touch and kiss me even though I asked him to stop. At this point, I remembered that even though I grew up with a very loving family, on a pretty safe block, I knew how to check a man really quickly and if needed inflict some real pain. So, I decided to let him know that I was capable of cutting him and would have no problem doing so. With that, he let me go. I never spoke to him again. You would think that was enough for me to be careful with whom I spent my time with, right? Nope. At that time I still hadn't learned. This next experience that I am going to share with you most definitely woke me up.

Because I was dealing with poor self-image and low self-esteem, I found myself surrounded by people I really didn't like. I spent time with them because they gave me attention. This was with all of my friendships and relationships. Now, all of this sounds really crazy because I enjoyed being around people. I mean I was elected class secretary for both my freshman and sophomore years. I was involved in countless campus activities, groups and ministries. I always had a large group of friends around me, but . in all of that I still felt alone. And because I was always the bigger girl in the group, whatever positive attention I received I ran with. I met this Atlanta police officer when I was 17. He had to have been at least 32 or so. He picked me up from my dorm and took me back to his condo. I was mesmerized. His condo had a city skyline view and a balcony. When we were sitting outside at about 2:00 a.m., I realized that I had no business being there with him and I definitely didn't want to go through with having sex, which is what he had picked me up for. I asked him to take me home. He refused. But because he was 32 and not 18, he knew to threaten me before I even thought to scream. He said that he would take me home when he got ready. About every 30 minutes I would ask as sweetly as I could if he was ready and I would continue to be ignored. About 11 am the next morning, he finally told me to get ready. I didn't sleep at all that night. I was afraid of what he would have done to me. I thought about leaving many times that night while he drifted off to sleep but I had no clue where I was or how to get back to my dorm. I was also afraid that he would make good on his threats. So I sat, waited, and prayed. He finally took me back and I decided then, low self-esteem or not, I wasn't running off with any strange men again.

Reflection:

As I reflect, what I have learned is that growing up and coming of age doesn't have to be a race. Slow down! It is okay to take your time and ease into becoming an adult. Believe me; you will be an adult a lot longer than you will be a teenager. Don't rush it. Be wary of those who try and convince you to do things outside of your comfort zone, especially if the push isn't for something that is going to help you be better or greater. Coming of age and growing up is a beautiful experience and one that is going to come with its own set of challenges. Life doesn't need you to help it along! Take your time and be thoughtful of the people you spend time with and the decisions you make. Make sure it's good stuff that follows you.

I had a few scary incidents that I allowed my insecurities and low self-esteem to place me in. That doesn't have to be your story! Don't allow yourself to be rushed into adulthood, not even by yourself. My desire is that this letter gives you the push you need to grow at a pace that is appropriate for you and your journey!

. . . .

Dear Little Sister:

Becoming a woman and learning to handle the responsibility of the freedom that womanhood brings, is overrated sometimes! Seriously, there is so much that you are expected to know when you hit this magical number of 18. I know women in their 40s that still haven't figured it out. So, please take the pressure off of yourself. What you need to know will manifest itself when it is time to implement that knowledge. Knowing who you are is a life-long journey. Yes, there are a few bedrock principles that you will identify sooner than later, but who you are will transform as you experience life and all that it brings. Give yourself grace. Grace is what you need when you ask someone for forgiveness and they grant it because they believe that your intent was not to hurt or disappoint them. We have to learn how to give ourselves grace as well when we disappoint ourselves. Believe me. I beat myself up about decisions I made. I had lot of regrets. But I decided to forgive myself and give myself some grace or room to make mistakes again without the pain of shame attached to my life. I want you to do the same. Live life and and then forgive yourself for any mistakes you may make--and you wilJust get up and try again.

Here's an affirmation for you to declare. Say it until you believe it!

Will you learn to trust yourself and give yourself time to grow up?

I owe no one an explanation when I say no. I am able to say no without any guilt.

. . . .

Chapter Nine

Built for a Father's Love

There is always a ram in the bush.
– Henry Venning

Father-daughter relationships are unique. The relationship between a daughter and her father usually set the tone for her relationships with men. Good or bad. When I think of my Daddie, I always smile. I can't help it. He was a great man. Daddie. I remember when Beyonce' released a song on her <u>Dangerously in Love</u> album. It was called "Daddy". Here is a stanza that resonates the most with me:

"Because you loved me I overcome
And I'm so proud of what you've become
You've given me such security
No matter what mistakes I know you're there for me
You cure my disappointments and you heal my pain
You understood my fears and you protected me
Treasure every irreplaceable memory and that's why… "

This song right here always brings to my mind vivid memories I shared with my Daddie. When I miss him the most, this is the soundtrack that I close my eyes to. My tears then become captured by my smile.

I was your quintessential Daddy's girl! Where he went, that's where I was going. Daddie was my security blanket. I knew all was okay in the world as long as I was with Daddie. I promise you, Beyonce' and I are kindred spirits! I mean, except the Bayou and the tattoos, these lyrics could have come from my journal. My

Mommie teases me that I am still unmarried because I am looking for someone with my father's qualities and she is absolutely right. I know how incredibly blessed I am. So many little girls didn't grow up with their fathers and then there are little girls whose fathers were present, but didn't make them feel special or like they could conquer the world. My Daddie did all of that for me. He was my very own superhero. He always made whatever I wanted and needed happen, with no questions asked.

Daddie was 54 when I was born. Growing up my friends assumed he was my grandfather and I would proudly correct them. I mean their thirty-something Daddies weren't riding bikes backwards down the block, or playing volleyball with them and their cousins. Their daddies weren't letting them climb onto their shoulders and try and braid their hair (he had this thick curly hair). Their daddies weren't taking them fishing and crabbing or building them their very own two- story playhouse for them and their friends. But, my Daddie was and I was so proud of him. Wherever he went, I was right there behind him. I just knew he was going to live forever. He had to.

As I grew older I came to terms with the fact that maybe he wasn't going to be around as long as I wanted him to be. I just knew that I needed to make the most of the time we had together. Now, I mostly just have memories. After my freshman year of college, I returned home that summer of 1999. My college best friend was flying to meet me in Virginia Beach. She was going to help me drive back. While we were waiting her to arrive that week, I went to have a few checkups. Even though I was 18, I still took one of my parents with me to the doctor's office. My mother went with me to my routine yearly visit at the gynecologist. A few days later I received a call to come in to have my test results read. Since I was 10 and had started my cycle, my pap smears were always abnormal. I figured this was just a routine visit. Daddie and I went. My life changed that day. The doctor told me that I had cervical dysplasia and that it was severe enough that if it went untreated I would be facing cervical cancer at eighteen years old. I was literally one step away on a chart. At 18, that is some scary stuff! Daddie just sat there and then he finally asked what we needed to do. The doctor scheduled an outpatient procedure and we went home to tell Mommie.

I will never forget that day. We sat around the dining table in the den. Daddie and I began to tell Mommie what the doctor shared and what we needed to do. Mommie got quiet and then she and Daddie began to tell me his prostate cancer was back. Back?! When did he have it before? They begin to remind me of the time he was in the hospital when I was about eleven years old. I thought he was just having tests done. Now, I was dealing with my own health scare, Daddie out of remission cancer, and my Mommie had to deal with both her husband and her only child having cancer at the same time. I was admitted for an outpatient surgery the following day I was told the surgery was routine, and I would be in and out in about six hours, tops. I could even prepare to leave to return to Atlanta the following day. I was already nervous, but we prayed and I was reminded that this was a normal and routine procedure to remove the cancerous cells and possibly shorten my cervix a bit to ensure that all of the area that was affected was out of my body. My doctor had done this numerous times. I remember lying on the table and being given anesthesia. I was told to count backwards from 100. I don't remember getting past 97. When I finally awoke, I was tied to the bed by my wrists with a tube down my throat to help me breathe. I couldn't breathe. I was in Intensive Care. This is where you go when the doctor's believe your condition is critical and they are unsure as to how you are going to respond to their treatments. This is where I woke up., not in the outpatient recovery room as expected.

When I opened my eyes my family was standing around me: my Mommie and Daddie, my Godfather, and my Daddie's best friend, and my childhood pastor and his wife. They were praying and I was wondering what in the hell had happened. I tried to talk and realized I couldn't. I went to pull the tube out of my mouth and realized that both hands were tied to the bed. I was stuck. I couldn't even ask what was wrong or what had happened. I could only blink my eyes. There was a really sweet nurse who was super patient with me as I made motion to have the tube removed and she reminded me that I needed it to breathe. It hurt and it was challenging to breathe because I also had to vomit through this same tube. It wasn't a great situation.

Afterwards, I learned that during the procedure, I began to awake and the anesthesiologist began to pump more anesthesia in me to make me go back to sleep. Well, this completely freaked out my doctor/surgeon and in the middle of the procedure she just started crying. They had to call in another doctor to finish the procedure while the anesthesiologist was still trying to give me enough so I wouldn't feel any pain. Between trying to calm down my doctor, get a new doctor in and keep me asleep, someone forgot to monitor what I was getting and how much. They gave me too much and I developed pulmonary edema., meaning I was literally drowning. My lungs were full of fluid and I couldn't breathe. I spent two nights in ICU before being moved to a private room. Mommie and Daddie were right there, along with all of my family. I had so many visitors. I felt so loved. Another doctor came in and his first words to me were, "I am here to clean up the mess." Now, I was scared. He began to share with us what happened, that my lungs shut down and began to fail. This is why I couldn't breathe. Oxygen couldn't get into to be able to breathe at 100% again. I spent five days in the hospital before I could leave for home.

What is even more crazy about this story is that they gave me so much anesthesia that when they came out of the operating room to give my parents and family an update, they told my parent's to prepare for my funeral. They told my Mommie and Daddie that their baby girl wasn't going to make it. That it was over. Little did they know that there was a grander plan for my life. This is one of the experiences that forced me to discover what my purpose is. I had another chance at life and I wanted to do something special with it. I spent another week at home and Daddie and I hit the road to Atlanta.

I hate how Daddie ended up driving me back to Atlanta, but I was so grateful for the time. It was just me and him on the road in my little red Neon. I drove a lot of the way. I could tell Daddie was tired. But he kept me up with his tall tales and stories of his childhood like he would normally do. We stopped for bacon and egg sandwiches, boiled peanuts, pork rinds, and strawberry pies! He got me to Atlanta safely and all checked into my dorm. He made sure all of my belongings were in my room and then we went to dinner. Thank God that this was before 9/11 because when I dropped him off at the airport I was able to walk him all the way to the gate and wait with him. I could tell that he just wanted to rest. I grabbed a newspaper for him and some snacks and was prepared to wait until the plane took off. However, Daddie made me leave. He said it was dark and didn't want me driving on the road at night. I told him Daddie drove at night all the time and I wanted to stay with him. Truthfully, I didn't want to leave my him at all. In his thick Gullah accent and dialect, Daddie said "Awww den, but I told ya to go." (The 'den' part makes sense if you Gullah/Geechee). So I kissed Daddie, went back to my dorm and awaited the phone call from Mommie saying that she had picked him up safely.

Reflection:

I would end up driving home every other month to make sure I saw my Daddie. He was getting sicker and was taking his chemotherapy treatments. I remember the first time I went home and saw all of his thick curly salt and pepper hair gone. He had one of my uncles come and shave his head. He preferred to cut it off before chemo took it. He had lost weight but was still determined to get up and do something. I liked taking him to chemo when I was home. Being sick didn't keep Daddie from being the life of the party. Even at his therapy appointments he was telling stories and turning on the charm. Mommie was good because these nurses were in their flirting with her man! Daddie was never disrespectful; he was just full of life, confident. We weren't' using this term back then, but my Daddie had swag. Just him entering the room made it light up. You felt different when you were around him. He had the ability to make you feel good even if you didn't know why.

Daddie made the decision to stop chemo sometime in the Spring of 2000 but the cancer didn't go away. He was ready. He had lived a long life. He raised some awesome children, gave Mommie the 20 years of marriage he promised her, built a lasting legacy and he made peace that he had fulfilled his purpose. Daddie lived life on purpose, and even though he was wheel- chair bound, by July he made it a priority to attend my older sister's wedding in Ft. Lauderdale, FL. You should have seen me wheeling him in the airport past security because they wanted to admit him to the hospital on our return home. I said, "NOPE! My Daddie is going home with me."

I returned to school in August of 2000 ready to begin my Junior year of college. Every day I waited for the phone to ring and for my Mommie to be on the other side telling me Daddie was gone. I called every day and most days he couldn't talk long with me or talk at all. Mommie called the week I was supposed to take finals. I immediately jumped in the car and drove home with my college best friend. She tried to convince me to wait. I explained to her that my Mommie called to say Daddie was calling for his children. She understood and said if I was going she was going too. Here we were ditching finals to go and see about my Daddie. She got me there safely and upon entering Mommie and Daddie's bedroom, he Daddie looked up and said, "So you brought 'her' with you?" We laughed because at least we knew he remembered us. My college best friend left the next day so she could get back to school. I stayed home caring nothing about class, grades or a test.

The days went by and Daddie got worse. His hospice nurse would just sit and read to him every day. I didn't think Daddie was going to make it through Christmas, but we went and bought him pajamas as a gift. By now he wasn't talking much. And his memory was fading. But he always remembered me, my name, that I was his baby. The man lying before me wasn't the Daddie I knew. I didn't know this helpless, lifeless man. I tried hard to prepare for his death. While I was coming home that Thanksgiving I had written him a letter. I read it to him during that time. I thanked him for being an awesome and a one- of -a-kind father. I told him that my life and my perspective on men and how I am to be treated was set by the tone he provided and by the example he gave in how he loved my mother and his children, both blood and adopted.

Daddie died on December 29, 2000 in the early morning. I remember waking up the very moment he took his last breath and just waited for Mommie to come and get me. We made the necessary phone calls and waited for the funeral home to come and get his body. Our house was swarming with family, friends, people. I slept a lot during that time. I thought I was strong and had accepted what had just disappeared from my life. The very first person I loved unconditionally had died. But my sorrow was almost immediately replaced with awe at his Homegoing Service. It was standing room only in our home church that sat 350 people. The choir stand was full. When it was time for others to make remarks, I will never forget this unsuspecting young man who stood up to speak. He was Daddie's total opposite. Daddie was this old, lovable black man who worked with his hands daily. Here was this very young white man who was dressed in a suit so he could immediately go to his office job after the service. When he stood up he said, "I only met Mr. Venning one time at a store. But he changed my life in that one instance. I saw his obituary in the paper and told me wife that I had to go. He was special and I am so very sorry for your loss. That one five minute conversation changed me to want to become a better man. I want to live a life like Mr. Venning's." That young man never mentioned what the conversation was and I don't think I thought to go and ask him. But here was this stranger confirming everything we had already known. Daddie's purpose in life wasn't just to build houses and structures. His purpose was to build lives. And he did it each and every day.

I could go on and on about my Daddie, it's easy for me to, but the thing I want you to take from my sharing this experience is that once you realize who and what you are, living life is easy. And it makes the lives of those around you easier too. See, when life got too hard and we wondered how or when something would happen, Daddie would remind us that there is "always a ram in the bush". You may know this story from the Bible with Abraham and his son, but if not, what that phrase symbolizes is that there is always going to be a way made. Your resources are always going to present themselves when necessary. Take no worry of how and why. Just be prepared. And I would need that reminder after Daddie died. I often wonder how we were going to make it and each and every time I began to doubt, God would send a resource to provide exactly what I was wanting from my Daddie.

Losing a parent is a horrible feeling, whether you are close to them or not. But to a little girl who has dreams of her Daddie walking her down the aisle or holding her through her first real heart break, losing her father can be crushing. Take the opportunity you have now to relish in the moments you have left and if your father has already passed or maybe you don't have a relationship with your living father, know that God wants to bring someone to you if your open that will give you the love you seek that only a daddy can give. I pray that this letter helps you mend your broken heart, strengthen your existing relationship or learn how to smile at the memories.

Dear Little Sister:

I am not naïve enough to believe that every little girl had a father in her life. If you didn't, I hate that you missed out on the opportunity to experience the love that a Daddie gives to her daughter. But what I will say to you is that if you are open, there is someone who can appropriately love you and pour into your life. A lot of times we decide that we don't want something because it isn't showing up in the manner in which we thought it would come. We reject good things and good people because they aren't attached to the things and people we want, good or bad. Allow yourself to be loved appropriately by someone who wants good things for you. There is something that as a young woman you need that only a father or a father figure can give you. They are our first teachers on how we are to be treated, respected and loved. If your Daddie is around, and he's present and loving, grow closer to him and challenge him to be better. Call your Daddie often. They do better when we are upfront and honest about what we need from them. Let your Daddie be there for you. Let him pick up some of your broken pieces and make sure he knows that there is a place for him in your life. Let your Daddie be your superhero.

Here's an affirmation for you to declare. Say it until you believe it!

Will you allow room for your Father's love?

I am open to receive the love I need and desire from my father.

Chapter Ten

Built for This

I was built to conquer everything meant to break me.
I was built for this!
– KaCey Venning

Getting to 35 has been hard work! And 35 is not old. There is still a lot of life left for me to live. However, my desire is that it doesn't take you this long to figure it out. Even as I am writing this, there are tears in my eyes. Why? Because as far as I have come, there is still some work left for me to do and I am not saying that had I started earlier living in my purpose that I would be "done, but I do believe I would have saved a lot of time, money , and heartache. But, it's okay, because each decision has a purpose. Each day is an opportunity to learn and to grow. Each day brings an opportunity to become better than you were the day before. I have become more aware that my life has meaning and I learn more and more about what I am supposed to do with this meaning every day. We hear it and it can be a bit cliché at times, but it's a very true statement: "Your life has meaning." Not only does my life have meaning, but so does yours.

This book was a labor of love, not just for you, but for me as well. See, I was afraid to write this book because I was deathly afraid of what others would think. Would people approve of it and what I had to say? With all of the work that I had done internally, I still wondered if my voice had any meaning. Would people laugh at me or talk about me? Was this something I wasn't supposed to do because others in my circle had done something similar? Never mind the fact that I sat on most what of my ideas and desires because I was afraid and far too consumed with what others had to say. I was very comfortable playing in the background. I enjoyed helping others accomplish their goals. It made me feel as though I was contributing something great by making sure others shined. And that's okay. We all need someone who is going to support us and fill in the gaps while we are on our way to greatness. But, I kept wondering if maybe I hadn't heard my own voice enough to make a decision on how my purpose was supposed to play in the world. However, what helped shift my thinking was when I realized that a lot of those same people weren't willing or able to support me in the same way.

Now, let me be clear. We can't go around doing things for people in hopes that they will do something for us. That is an awesome and guaranteed way to get your feelings hurt! We serve and help others because it's the right thing to do. But, we all need a support system too. Make sure you are helping because you want to and not look for it to come from those you have served and helped. Really, it's okay. You are sowing seeds and your harvest will come. But, I digress. I also became aware that I was okay in the background because I wasn't completely sure of who I was or wanted to be. I didn't know the sound of my own voice. I am sure you picked up on some of that in the earlier chapters. When you don't know who, what, whose or why you are, it's easy to run with someone else's dream. Another consequence of this is the time you waste on other's dreams that you could be using to propel your own. You know what else happens when you don't know who you are? You constantly find yourself doing what feels good in the moment of what's trending, what has worked for others. The difference between doing something that is similar and popular and being considered a fraud or a duplicate is YOU! Two people can do the same two things, but when you know who you are, there is something different about how others receive, perceive, and accept you and what you have to offer the world. What's that something extra that only you can give the familiar?

You are an individual piece of the world and your piece is needed in order to complete the larger puzzle. I firmly believe that we are here on this earth for something specific. There is something that only you can do in a specific way. The hard work is finding out and remembering what that specific purpose is. What is it that you are designed to do? What were you wonderfully created for? What is your life's purpose? You aren't too young or ever too old to figure it out. What can you boldly declare you were built for? Maybe it's singing, or art. It could be ministry, nonprofit and volunteer work or business. Maybe you hold the cure to cancer or HIV/AIDS? Just maybe you will write the next great classic novel or revolutionize the way we use technology. What is it? Once you know, it's time to move in that direction. As you continue to grow and mature you will realize that your purpose doesn't change, just the way you package it and deliver it to the world. Writing this for you, it was clear to me. I have always been a helper. And I have always had an opportunity to use my voice. But each stop in my journey had me present it differently. As long as I am firm and sure that what I am doing is helping others and that I have an opportunity to use my voice in the process, I am still aligned with what I am supposed to be and purposed to do.

I enjoy studying Oprah Winfrey. She figured out her purpose, carved a niche and decided to live confidently in it. One of my favorite observations of hers is when she shares her "What I know for sure" segments. These are bedrock principles that she lives by and it brings about a manifestation of blessings, opportunities and growth in her life. What I know for sure is that I was built to overcome EVERTYHING meant to destroy me. What I shared in this book is just a glimpse into pieces of it. What I know for sure is that I am stronger than I think. I have something amazing to offer this world and allowing my fears, insecurities and self-doubt does nothing but shortchange myself and others! Yes, think about it. What if I allowed my fears to continue to overtake me? You wouldn't be reading the words on these pages or experiencing a breakthrough of your own. I learned that I have been aware of my purpose and my gift all along. I just didn't know what to do with it. I didn't think it was intriguing or "sexy" enough. The one thing

I do well, without having to try hard, is help others. I am also called upon to speak and talk a lot. Mostly, because I enjoy it, but speaking in front of large crowds don't scare me. So, I needed to figure out how to merge the two together. I wanted to make sure my life was dedicated to helping others and that I could use my voice in the process. Believe me; my experiences weren't just for me. They were for me to go through so you wouldn't feel alone or have to suffer as much.

Helping Empower Youth, Inc. was created in to help others, young people specifically. It was designed and purposed to provide an opportunity for young people to find and use their voices. Co-founding and managing a nonprofit has been some of the hardest work I have ever done. The work that I do with young people forces me to be authentic and sincere. It forces me to use my voice daily as an example. But, my nonprofit and volunteer work also makes me ever so mindful of who I am and what others miss out on when I shrink into the corner or allow my insecurities to control my voice and my life. You too, have something great to give the world and you will be doing me a disservice if you choose not to ignite the passion and fire that lives in you. Walk in your purpose. Identify and understand what your "this" is and loudly declare, "I AM BUILT FOR THIS!" My "what I know for sures" have become my Built for This mantras. This is what I tell myself when I am discouraged, feeling defeated or unsure of the next step. I want to share them with you.

Who knew life would be so many ups and downs? And a lot of it will make you seem like you can't handle it. Here's a secret… you absolutely can! You are designed to accomplish great things and you are built to handle it all. I pray this letter reminds you of your greatness and how incredibly strong you are.

Dear Little Sister:

Built for this was born out of my need to have a short reminder that I can handle life. I bet you are wondering what the "this" is though. I wondered about that for a while too. The one thing that I can guarantee for you is that if you want to, you can make sure every life's experience, good or bad, is one that creates building blocks for your future. Over the past three years, I have learned that even the life experiences that were meant and sent to break me, in fact built me up. Those experiences built me to be stronger, more intuitive, more impactful, and more purposeful. And I want you to find something that helps you do the same! Here is what I know for sure: You owe it to yourself to identify and understand how strong you are, mentally, physically, emotionally and spiritually. I can't promise that life won't send some other "stuff" your or our way, but I can promise that there are tools we can use at any age and at any stage in our lives to take that "stuff" and STAND on it. Get ready to boldly declare," I AM BUILT FOR THIS!"

Here's an affirmation for you to declare. Say it until you believe it!

Are you ready to declare what you are built for?

Right now I love the person I am becoming and all I have to offer this world.

Acknowledgements

To my Mommie, Joyce C. Venning, I LOVE YOU MORE than all the words in every book you have ever read or written, and that's a lot!

To my Carroll and Venning families, I have been so incredibly blessed to be a part of such loving, distinctive and unique families. I am proud to call you mine.

Morning Star Baptist Church, thank you for being my extended family then and now. Thank you for your prayers and support. I would also like to thank my Beechwood family. You provided the backdrop to a life that can't be written about fully, only lived.

Roderick and Ilka Murray, never in a million years would I have imagined the impact that two people could make on someone's life. I love you two so very much and I am honored and privileged to call you both Pastor and friend.

To Shalena D.I.V.A. Broaster, thank you for being excited from the beginning. Thank you for providing the opportunity for me to learn a bit more about what I am built for and to place it in a format others could read.

To those who I call sister and brother, both blood and by choice, my Circle of 100, my 3 godsister/sisterfriends, to those who walk with me daily as my best friend and family, to those who have listened to my cries, wiped away my tears, held my hand and reminded me that I was worthy, thank you!

About the Author

KaCey is a product of a family rooted in living out their purpose. From to business to education and the advancement of youth people to intellectuals to ministry, she has always found herself thrust into the middle of helping other sort their "stuff" out too. KaCey has been a sought after leader and speaker since she was a youth and she has used this gift of leadership and communication to empower and encourage people of all ages to be the change they want to see in the World. KaCey has been able to facilitate this work as a teacher, a nonprofit professional and founder, a National Service member and as a ministry leader.

KaCey thrives from speaking, teaching and facilitating opportunities for others to realize their purpose and to help provide tools to help them actualize their gift to the others. She has done this through her work professionally with Fortune 500 companies such as Coca-Cola, L'Oreal Paris USA, Scholastic and Home Depot. She has helped to foster custom Cause Marketing and Corporate Social Responsibility Plans for companies and small businesses alike. But KaCey has also learned how to translate her approach to corporations to individuals by helping them identify their own Corporate Social Responsibility Plan or better known as your purpose.

KaCey holds a Bachelor's of Arts Degree in Sociology and is the Co-Founder of Helping Empower Youth, Inc.